GNOMES OF THE SILVER SCREEN

GNOMES OF THE SILVER SCREEN

DAVID W. WATTS

ROBSON
BOOKS

Produced 2005 by
PRC Publishing,
The Chrysalis Building
Bramley Road, London W10 6SP

An imprint of **Chrysalis** Books Group plc

First published in Great Britain in 2005 by
Robson Books
The Chrysalis Building
Bramley Road, London W10 6SP

An imprint of **Chrysalis** Books Group plc

1 2 3 4 5 6 7 8 9

ISBN: 1 86105 857 8

Printed in China

INTRODUCTION
Gnome Film Making – A Retrospective

Each year in Hollywood the great and the good of the film world gather to hear the results of a vote by members of The Academy of Motion Pictures, Arts and Science. Inside the Kodak Theater, the Oscar nominations are read out and the small statuettes are duly awarded to a stream of suitably emotional winners. It is an event that is beamed across the globe and reported universally in the media of the Western world. The fact that the ceremony celebrates only a fraction of the planet's annual film output is largely glossed over.

Cinema is not an American invention, but a French one, and it is now the Indian subcontinent which produces and watches a larger proportion of films than Hollywood turns out each year. For many years the Bollywood phenomenon

Right: Barley Chapmin in his famous role as The Trumper.

was overlooked by Western cinema-goers, but now Indian directors are being celebrated for developing a unique artform that is enjoyed by over a billion people.

If Bollywood found itself on the margins in the past, there is an even more neglected genre to be discovered in the future. Little publicity has been given to films produced by small, bearded, red-capped figures often found decorating suburban gardens. But gnome cinema has been around since the turn of the century—from when August Lumière first left some spare equipment in an outside shed—yet few movie buffs can claim to have seen even one gnome motion picture.

Gnomes of the Silver Screen sets out to show movie buffs exactly what they have been missing. Dig (or fork gently) below the surface of conventional cinema and you will find a parallel universe of gnome cinema, which takes the plots of popular films and adapts them to reflect gnome lives, gnome loves and gnomic values.

As the Americans developed the silent movies, so gnome films sprung into life in the early twentieth century. These were one reel, mainly comic films starring notable stars of the era, such as Barley Chapmin and Mabel Gnomin.

By the late 1920s the talkies had arrived in potting sheds in gardens everywhere and eager gnomes flocked to see breathrough movies such as *The Jazz Sprinkler*, *King Gnome* and Walt Bisley's first ever animated feature, *The Snow White Giant*.

Once the talkies had become familiar fare, gnomes thrilled to see the first technicolour movies where vivid red boots, verdant green grass and bright blue trousers erupted from the screen in such epics as *Gnome with the Wind*. Musicals became popular; for the first time big stage performances could be seen combining song and dance routines with potting up and pricking out.

Gnome cinema developed its legends too. Every living gnome has seen *Casablanca* starring Humphrey Handcart and there are few who would not recognise the classic line: "Of all the garden centres, in all the world, you have to walk into mine."

Following World War II, the popularity of television saw the mass appeal of gnome cinema diminish as television began to steal audiences away from the big screen. For the first time gnome film makers turned to shock tactics to appeal to a younger, teenage audience. There was a near riot at the film premiere of *Psickle*, the movie in which sad and lonely Gnomin Bates lures innocent women to spend the night at the Bates Windmill.

The 60s and 70s witnessed the rise of cult cinema. Gnomey Twobricks' depiction of *A Clockwork Turnip* was banned on its first release; the sight of so many raw root

Right: Gnome superstar Hugh Plant, star of Brit hits,
Gloves Actually *and* Four Weddings and a Water Wheel.

long planks
shaving ryan's privets
r.u.bish burns   mat damson   tom sizeless

vegetables proving too much for the film censor. Twobricks went on to direct many important red-cap movies, such as *The Shining Gnome* and *2001: A Spade Odyssey*. However, numbers at the box office still continued to decline.

That's not to say there weren't some must-see movies that grossed big numbers at the shed door. Film director Stephen Spielbud had a string of spectacular successes in the 70s and 80s with *Chores*, *G.T.* (the gnome terrestrial), *Indiana Bonemeal and the Traders of the Lost Bark* and his groundbreaking film that re-wrote the rulebook on pruning movies, *Shaving Ryan's Privets*.

In the late twentieth and early twenty-first century, potting sheds reported audiences returning to watch a new wave of younger film directors replacing the auteur gnomes of the past. *Reservoir Gnomes,* featuring Mr Tulip, Mr Snowdrop, Mr Crocus, Mr Lupin and Mr Bluebell was an impressive debut for Quentin Tarantula. The director went on to even greater triumph at the 2005

Watering Can Festival winning five Golden Globe Artichokes for *Till Bill*, a story of ultimate revenge and hoeing.

Now, to celebrate a century of gnome movies, *Gnomes of the Silver Screen* has drawn together for the first time some of the best-known film posters of the last 100 years. A whole new audience can learn about the history of this much-loved and much-neglected branch of film making; an art form where the term post-modern means plastic gnome, not ceramic.

David W. Watts

April 2005

9½ Leeks

They broke every trowel

GNOMEY TWOBRICK'S

CLOCKWORK TURNIP

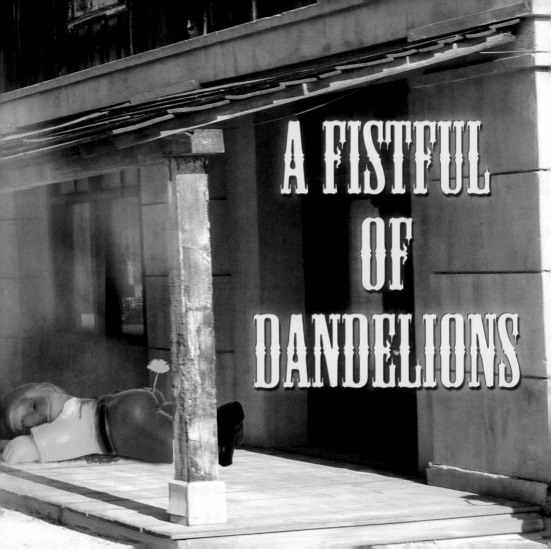

AMERICAN **GNOMEY**

...don't look closer

...and don't forget to clean the pond

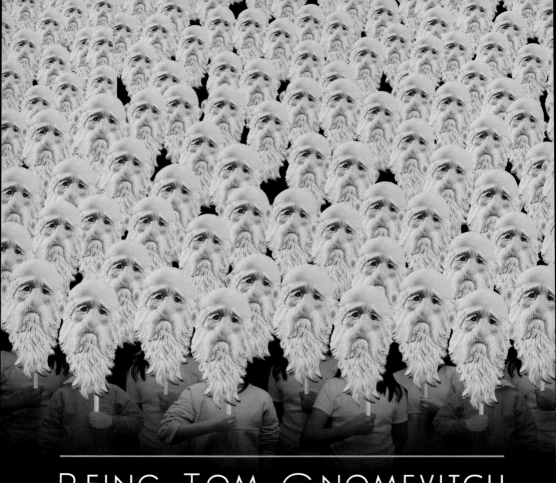

BEING TOM GNOMEVITCH

THE BRIAR GNOME PROJECT

SMELL TWIGSON
BRAVEFART

'They may take away our chives,

but they'll never take OUR FREESIAS!'

NO FISHING RODS • NO SPADES •

CHAMPIGNON

Nowal King (ON THE GRASS)
CHILDREN OFF THE LAWN
And a gnome shall lead them

From the author of The Dead Gnome
Bonfire Starter
Salem's Plot
The Green Pile
Pot Sematary
The Bark Half

Le nain en

Chocolat

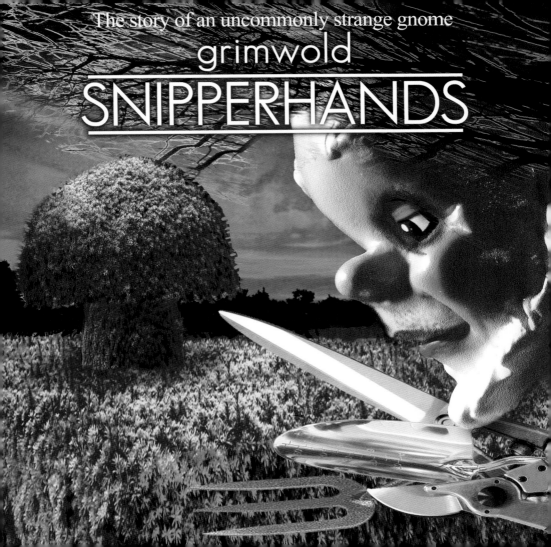

JUST WHEN YOU THOUGHT IT WAS SAFE TO GO BACK IN THE POND AND HAVE A BREAK FROM THOSE . .

CHORES

CITIZEN CANE

The name of his wheelbarrow...was Rosebug

IN A GREENHOUSE NO ONE CAN HEAR YOU SCREAM

Inside everyone is a dance routine waiting to be discovered...

The Badger Pack Gathers

DIRTY HAIRY

I know what you're thinking. "Did he use ten squirts or only nine?"
Well, to tell you the truth, sixlegs, in all this excitement I kinda' lost track mysel
But seeing as this is 'Bugmelt', the most powerful insecticide in the world,
and would blow your head clean off, you've got to ask yourself one question:
Do I feel lucky? Well, do ya . . . . . punk?

G.T.

PHONE GNOME

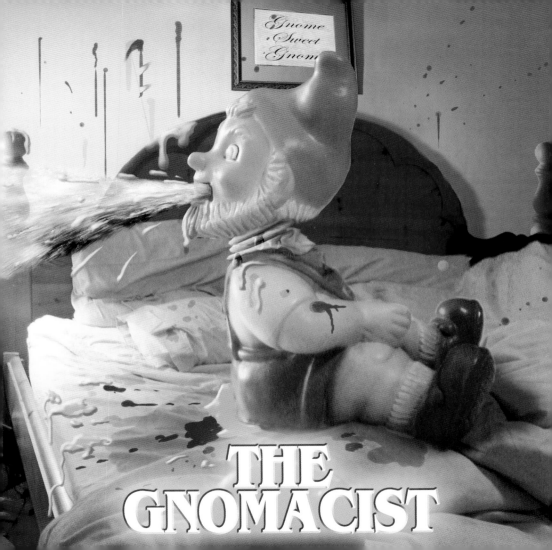

Gnome Sweet Gnome

THE GNOMACIST

He took her flowers
Now he's getting stalked

HOUSE OF GREEN

In the year 2005 the once powerful Pong Dynasty is having it's tulips dug up by rebel armies.

FLYING SWATTERS

From the director of 'Crouching Spider, Hidden Dragon Fly'

Forrest saves Fungi Dan

Woody
Planks is
Forrest
Dump

Drainspotting

Choose life. Choose a job.
Choose the garden centre toilets

GLADY

Father to a manicured lawn
Husbander to a mildewed rose
In this garden or the next,
I will have my vegetables!

ATOR

WHAT DID THE GNOMANS EVER DO FOR US?

THE GNOME'S POND . .
WURZEL POND

0.07ᴱ

LICENCE TO TILL

THERE IS A GNOMEBOT IN THIS FORMATION THAT DOES NOT BELONG, IDENTIFY IT!

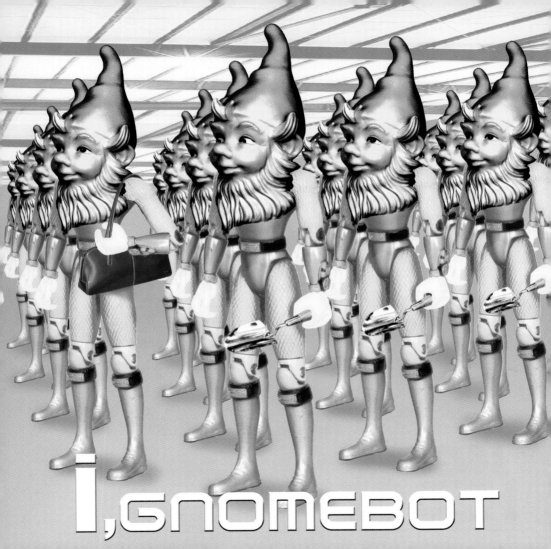

I,GNOMEBOT

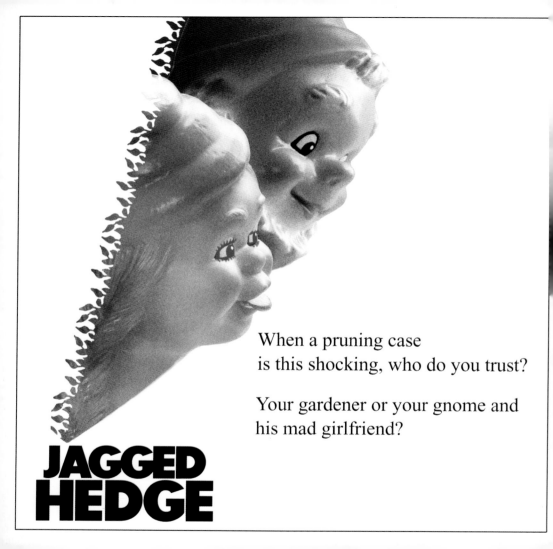

When a pruning case
is this shocking, who do you trust?

Your gardener or your gnome and
his mad girlfriend?

JAGGED HEDGE

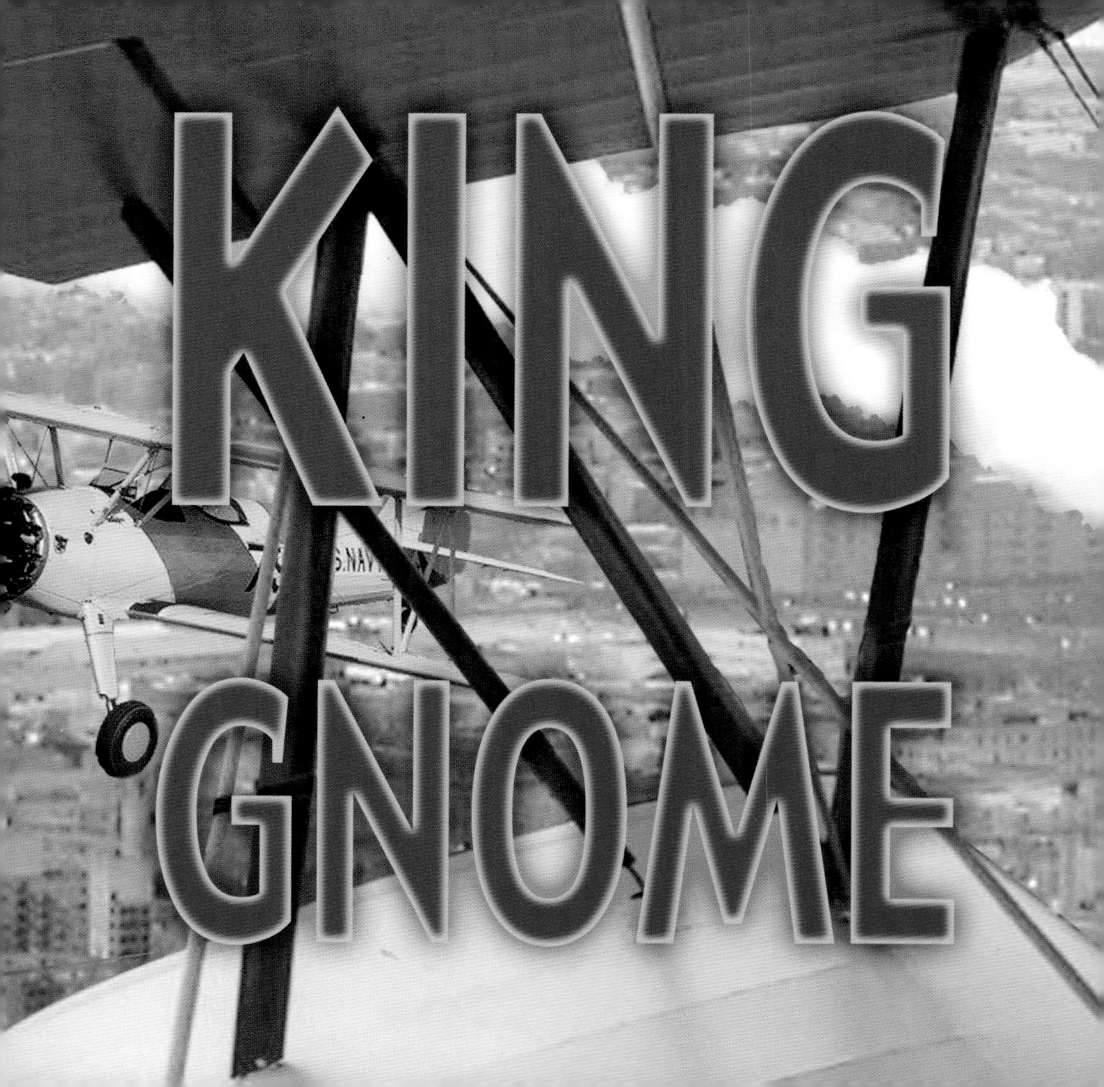
KING
GNOME
S.NAV

Lawrence *of a* DAHLIA

'ARRY WOZ HERE

Truly, for some gnomes nothing is written unless THEY write it.

PEARL'S

ARBOUR

reservoir gnomes

IT'S OFF TO WORK WE GO

ROCKERY

'You're gonna eat lichen' and you're gonna crap thunder!'

SATURDAY GNOME FEVER

FEVER

Where do you go when the gardening is over. . . .?

7 The Year Ditch

*A story of spades, digging
and cross-dressing in the shed*

long planks

shaving ryan's privets

r u bish burns   mat damson   tom sizeless

THE SILAGE OF THE GNOMES

THE
DRILLING
FIELDS

Here we must be like the mole, and have no thought, except for the Garden

Titus Sphincter :
   "I'm just going to water the snowdrops, I may be some time."

THE ANTARCTIC

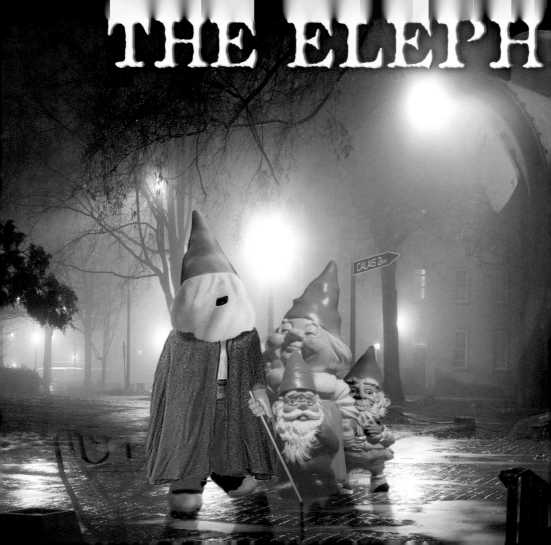

PHARTZENDIGGER

is

<u>THE GERMINATOR</u>
PLANTING DAY

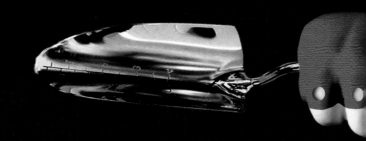

T H E
G N O M

GNOMEBASE

I need spades .

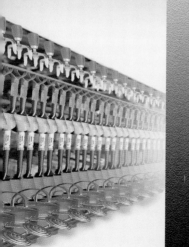

ETRIX

... lots of spades

GNOMEBASE

THE GREAT ESCAPE

Hours ago..minutes ago...these ornaments were behind panel fencing.

The Colored Purple Gnome

The Sodfather

LINE UP · NO WHEELBARROW

7"

6"

5"

4"

3"

Gnomes

THE 4TH PLOT BY QUATERPOUNDA TOMATOES

TILL
BILL

VOLUME 1

KILLUN DE GREENFLY

TERRY COTTA

WHYAR MESHIE

GnomeFellas

Three Decades of Life in the Garden

BARK GABLE   LEAFONNA TREE   LEAFY HOEWARD

GNOME WI

OLIVIN de GARDEN

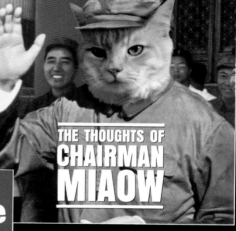